Agnès Varda

The Eye of Cinema

By

Charlotte Jane Fontaine

Table of contents :

INTRODUCTION

Cinema is an art form that can capture the human soul, delve into the depths of emotions, and tell stories that resonate with our own existence. Among the creators of this medium, few have succeeded in transcending cultural boundaries and touching the hearts of audiences as deeply and universally as Agnès Varda. This French filmmaker has left an indelible mark on cinema, not only in France but worldwide. Her unique body of work, bold vision, and charismatic personality have made her an iconic figure in the seventh art.

This book, "Agnès Varda: The Eye of Cinema," invites you to delve into the fascinating life and exceptional career of Agnès Varda. Throughout the pages, we will explore the multiple facets of this artist, from her humble beginnings in French cinema to international recognition, her advocacy for women's rights, and her ability to capture the essence of humanity through the lens of her camera.

Agnès Varda was not just a filmmaker but also a storyteller, a visionary, and a feminist who used cinema as a means of artistic and political expression. She revolutionized the cinematic landscape as part of the New Wave, a movement that reimagined storytelling on screen. However, her impact goes far beyond that vibrant era of French cinema. She continued to create innovative films and explore new artistic territories throughout her life, leaving behind a cinematic legacy that continues to inspire and influence future generations of filmmakers.

Beyond her cinematic career, this book will also unveil lesser-known aspects of Agnès Varda's personal life, from her family to her hobbies, encompassing the personal elements that shaped her art. You'll discover the actors and actresses who marked her career, the legendary moments of her life, and her status as a true cinema icon.

Through an in-depth exploration of her work, influence, and legacy, we will reveal why Agnès Varda remains an essential figure in world cinema. Whether you are a passionate cinephile, a fan of the New Wave, or simply curious to discover the life and work of an exceptional artist, this book offers a captivating journey through the world of Agnès Varda, a cinema pioneer who captured the soul of her time and continues to inspire future generations.

Get ready to explore the universe of Agnès Varda through her films and personal history, and discover why she rightfully remains "The Eye of Cinema."

Chapter 1: Childhood and Beginnings

Agnès Varda: An Unusual Childhood

To understand the essence of an artist, it is often essential to explore the roots of their personal history. In this chapter, we delve into the fascinating childhood of Agnès Varda, a period that shapes her unique perspective on the world and lays the groundwork for her future cinematic career.

Childhood in Belgium

Agnès Varda was born on May 30, 1928, in Ixelles, Belgium, into a family where art was a fundamental value. Her father, Eugène Jean Varda, hailing from Crete, brought a Greek touch to the family, while her mother,

Christiane Pasquet, was French. These diverse cultural influences contributed to broadening young Agnès's horizons from an early age.

Raised in an artistic and intellectual environment, Agnès Varda had the opportunity to mingle with artists and writers, nurturing her curiosity and creativity. It was here, in Belgium, that the first artistic impulses awakened, destined to leave an indelible mark on her future life.

Education and Early Passions

Agnès Varda's education was marked by insatiable curiosity. A precocious child, she was already interested in art, photography, and cinema. Her first forays into the art world were nourished by the richness of Brussels museums, where she spent long hours contemplating the works of the great masters.

However, it was photography that initially captured her attention. At the age of 18, she acquired her first camera and began exploring the world through her lens. This passion for photography would become a guiding thread throughout her life and be reflected in her later cinematic work.

Move to Paris

Agnès Varda's life takes a decisive turn when she decides to move to Paris to pursue her studies in the arts. It is in the French capital that she meets Jacques Demy, a man who would become her husband and artistic partner. This new environment, infused with French culture and its artistic effervescence, would play a crucial role in her career.

The First Film: "La Pointe Courte"

This chapter culminates with the creation of her first feature film, "La Pointe Courte" (1955). At the age of 27, Agnès Varda decides to venture into the world of cinema. With a modest budget and a small crew, she creates a film that would become a cornerstone of the New Wave, a revolutionary cinematic movement in France. Shot in Sète, the film tells the story of a couple in crisis, offering a poetic and innovative vision of reality.

The details of the challenges Agnès Varda faced in making "La Pointe Courte" and the initial reactions from critics and the public reveal the audacity and determination of a young director taking her first steps toward an exceptional cinematic career.

Through these accounts, we discover how Agnès Varda's childhood and her initial forays into the world of cinema were the prelude to an extraordinary artistic career. This chapter provides an intimate look at the beginnings of an artist who would leave an indelible mark on the history of French and global cinema through her boundless talent and creativity.

Chapter 2: The New Wave

The Impact of the New Wave on Agnès Varda's Work

The New Wave, the iconic cinematic movement of the 1950s and 1960s in France, had a profound impact on global cinema. Agnès Varda, one of its leading figures, plays an essential role in redefining cinematic language and exploring new narrative forms. In this chapter, we delve into the heart of this cinematic revolution and examine how the New Wave influences Agnès Varda's work.

The New Wave: A Cinematic Revolution

To understand the context in which Agnès Varda emerges as a director, let's explore the main characteristics of the New Wave. This movement is characterized by a break with traditional cinematic conventions, the use of lightweight cameras, the employment of non-professional actors, and the exploration of more personal and contemporary themes. The impact of the New Wave on French and international cinema is immense, and Agnès Varda is one of its most original voices.

Agnès Varda's Innovative Work

Next, let's explore Agnès Varda's filmography during the New Wave period. Her films, such as "Cléo from 5 to 7" (1962) and "Happiness" (1965), illustrate her commitment to new cinematic trends. We examine in detail how she incorporates key elements of the New Wave, such as realism, formal experimentation, and the exploration of human emotions, into her own work.

Collaborations with Other Iconic Directors

A fascinating aspect of this era is how directors collaborated and mutually influenced each other. Agnès Varda works alongside iconic New Wave directors such as François Truffaut and Alain Resnais. These collaborations enrich her work and bring a unique dimension to her films.

For example, her collaboration with François Truffaut on the film "The Little Soldier" (1963) shows how these two creative minds contributed to shaping contemporary French cinema. We see how their ideas and experiments translated to the screen and how these works left a mark on the history of cinema.

Furthermore, Agnès Varda collaborates with Alain Resnais on the short film "All the Memories in the World" (1956), exploring the National Library of France. This collaboration demonstrates the willingness to explore new cinematic territories and push the boundaries of storytelling.

By closely examining these partnerships, we can better understand the influence they had on French cinema at the time and how they contributed to the evolution of cinematic language.

This chapter invites you to dive into the creative effervescence of the New Wave and discover how Agnès Varda, with her distinctive style, contributes to this revolutionary movement. Her ability to integrate innovations of the time while preserving her personal artistic voice makes her an indispensable director of this pivotal period in cinema.

Chapter 3: The Visionary Feminist

Agnès Varda's Commitment to Women's Rights

Agnès Varda is not just a revolutionary filmmaker; she is also a pioneer in advocating for women's rights. In this chapter, we will explore her profound commitment to gender equality and how it manifested in her cinematic work.

Agnès Varda's Feminism

From the early days of her career, Agnès Varda has been a powerful voice in the feminist movement in France. She championed the idea that women should have an equal place in the film industry, both in front of and behind the camera. Her advocacy for diversity and the inclusion of women in cinema was ahead of its time, serving as a model for female filmmakers worldwide.

Her Engaged Films and Documentaries

Agnès Varda used cinema as a means to give a voice to women and shed light on gender issues. Through films like "One Sings, the Other Doesn't" (1977), she explores themes of sisterhood, maternity, and women's control over their own lives. This film, in particular, received acclaim for its authentic portrayal of women's struggles in society.

In her documentary "The Gleaners and I" (2000), Agnès Varda highlights women living on the fringes of society, often forgotten and invisible. This sensitive documentary provides a unique perspective on the female condition and the dignity of women struggling for survival.

The Role of Women in Her Body of Work

By delving deep into her films and documentaries, we will discover how Agnès Varda addressed issues of gender, sexuality, and identity in her work. Her cinematic oeuvre is a celebration of the diversity of female experiences, paving the way for a new generation of female filmmakers who continue to advance the cause of women in the film industry.

This chapter invites you to immerse yourself in Agnès Varda's passionate commitment to women's rights and explore how her feminist vision shaped her cinematic work, paving the way for a richer and more equitable representation of women on and behind the screen.

Chapter 4: Travels and International Influence

Agnès Varda's Journeys Around the World and Their Impact on Her Work

Agnès Varda was a filmmaker with an insatiable thirst for discovery and exploration. Her travels around the world played a significant role in shaping her artistic identity and deeply influenced her cinematic work. In this chapter, we delve into the world of Agnès Varda the globetrotter and examine how her journeys left their mark on her oeuvre.

Journey to South America: "Salut les Cubains" (1964)

One of Agnès Varda's most impactful journeys took her to South America, specifically to Cuba. Her documentary "Salut les Cubains" (1964) provides a unique glimpse into the Cuban revolution and the daily lives of its people. This journey profoundly influenced her cinematic approach, allowing her to capture the authenticity of the places and the people.

Trips to Africa: "Black Panthers" (1968) and "Lions Love (...and Lies)" (1969)

Agnès Varda also traveled to Africa, where she witnessed social and political movements of the time. Her documentary "Black Panthers" (1968) takes an uncompromising look at the Black Panthers movement in the United States, while "Lions Love (...and Lies)" (1969) explores the upheavals in American society during this period of cultural and political ferment. Her travels in Africa fueled her political sensibility and strengthened her commitment to documenting struggles for justice and equality.

Cultural and Artistic Influences

In addition to her documentary travels, Agnès Varda was influenced by cultures worldwide. Her open-mindedness and curiosity led her to explore various art forms, including photography and painting, in different parts of the globe. Artistic influences from afar enriched her cinematic language, enabling her to experiment with new techniques and push the boundaries of storytelling.

This chapter invites you to travel with Agnès Varda around the world and discover how her experiences and encounters profoundly influenced her cinematic work. Her ability to absorb and integrate foreign cultures into her art makes her a truly international filmmaker, whose work transcends geographical borders to resonate with a global audience.

Chapter 5: The Diversity of Her Filmography

An Overview of the Various Cinematic Genres Explored by Agnès Varda

Agnès Varda was a filmmaker of incredible versatility, and her filmography reflects this diversity. In this chapter, we will explore the multiple cinematic genres she delved into during her exceptional career.

Documentary: Capturing Reality

One of the most striking aspects of Agnès Varda's filmography is her commitment to documentary filmmaking. She used documentary cinema to explore important social and political subjects. Works such as "Le Bonheur" (1965), examining the life of a typical French family, or "Daguerréotypes" (1976), delving into the lives of Parisian shopkeepers, showcase her ability to sensitively and deeply capture reality.

Experimental Cinema: Pushing Boundaries

Agnès Varda also ventured into experimental cinema, pushing the limits of traditional storytelling. Her short film "La Jetée" (1962), a visual experiment in black and white, illustrates her desire to challenge cinematic conventions. This diversity of styles and approaches made her a pioneering filmmaker who was never afraid to take artistic risks.

Fiction Cinema: Narration and Creativity

In addition to documentary and experimental cinema, Agnès Varda directed fiction films that captivated audiences worldwide. Films such as "Cléo de 5 à 7" (1962), "Vagabond" (1985), and "The Beaches of Agnès" (2008) showcase her ability to tell complex stories and create memorable characters.

Recurring Themes in Her Work

While exploring her diversified filmography, we will also discover recurring themes that marked her work. The pursuit of truth, the human condition, the quest for self, and the ephemeral nature of life are recurring themes that consistently appear in her films. These universal themes allowed her work to resonate with a broad audience and influence many generations of filmmakers.

This chapter invites you to dive into the diversity of Agnès Varda's filmography, a filmmaker who dared to explore a multitude of cinematic genres while remaining true to her unique artistic voice. Her ability to navigate between different styles and express a variety of themes makes her a truly unforgettable director.

Chapter 6: The Actors and Actresses Who Shaped Her Career

Memorable Collaborations with Renowned Actors and Actresses

Agnès Varda had the privilege of working with numerous talented actors and actresses throughout her career, and these collaborations left an indelible mark on her cinematic oeuvre. In this chapter, we will explore the performers who contributed to enriching her films and the significance of their performances in her work.

Iconic Actors and Actresses in Her Films

Among the actors and actresses who left an impact on Agnès Varda's career are names synonymous with French and international cinema. Catherine Deneuve, who starred in "Les Créatures" (1966) and "Le Bonheur" (1965), stands out as one of Agnès Varda's most notable collaborators. Their artistic partnership gave rise to memorable films that were critically acclaimed.

Jacques Demy, the renowned director and Agnès Varda's husband, also played a significant role in her filmography. Their mutual influence contributed to shaping their respective styles and creating a lasting cinematic legacy.

The Importance of Performances in Her Films

Agnès Varda paid close attention to the quality of her actors' performances, often allowing them creative freedom to develop their characters. Her ability to guide actors while giving them room for expression resulted in authentic and moving interpretations.

In films such as "Vagabond" (1985), where Sandrine Bonnaire portrays a young homeless woman, or "Cléo de 5 à 7" (1962), with Corinne Marchand in the lead role, actresses' performances were praised for their depth and realism. Agnès Varda was a director who knew how to bring out the best in her actors, creating films that touched the hearts and souls of the audience.

This chapter invites you to discover the actors and actresses who contributed to Agnès Varda's exceptional cinematic legacy. Their memorable performances added an essential dimension to her work and helped establish her as one of the most respected directors in the history of cinema.

Chapter 7: International Recognition

Awards and Honors Received by Agnès Varda

Agnès Varda's career was adorned with success and accolades that bear witness to her immense talent as a filmmaker. In this chapter, we will delve into the awards and distinctions that marked her career, solidifying her status as an iconic figure in world cinema.

The Honorary Palme d'Or at the Cannes Film Festival

In 2015, Agnès Varda was honored by the Cannes Film Festival with the Honorary Palme d'Or for her entire body of work. This prestigious award acknowledges her impact on cinema and her influence on numerous generations of filmmakers. She became the first woman to receive this esteemed recognition.

The Honorary César Award

In 2001, she received the Honorary César Award, the highest honor in French cinema, in recognition of her outstanding contributions to the film industry. This distinction reflects her significance in French cinema and her contribution to the international cinematic scene.

The Honorary Academy Award (Oscar)

In 2017, Agnès Varda was bestowed with an Honorary Academy Award (Oscar) for her exceptional contribution to cinema. This recognition by the Academy of Motion Picture Arts and Sciences in the United States attests to her status as a world-renowned filmmaker.

Her Status as a Figure in World Cinema

Agnès Varda is not only a respected director but has also become an icon in world cinema. Her innovative work, boundless creativity, and ability to explore a variety of genres and themes have positioned her as a filmmaker whose influence transcends borders.

Her status as a cinema pioneer, committed feminist, and visionary artist is firmly established worldwide. She paved the way for numerous filmmakers and continues to inspire new generations of directors.

This chapter invites you to explore Agnès Varda's well-deserved international recognition—a filmmaker who left an indelible mark on the history of cinema, and whose impact continues to resonate globally.

Chapter 8: The Later Years

Her Work in the Final Years of Her Career

The latter years of Agnès Varda's career were marked by continued creativity and unwavering commitment to cinema. In this chapter, we will explore her late work, which attests to her constant passion for cinematic art.

Films of Maturity

Agnès Varda continued to create remarkable films throughout her life, including "The Beaches of Agnès" (2008), an autobiographical documentary reflecting on her career and personal life. This film was critically acclaimed and provided the audience with a deeper understanding of the artist behind the camera.

Reflections on Age and Death

In her later works, Agnès Varda explored themes related to age, mortality, and memory. Her short film "Faces Places" (2017), created in collaboration with the photographer JR, addresses the gradual fading of faces and memories as time passes. These films demonstrate her ability to evolve as a filmmaker and tackle universal subjects with heightened sensitivity.

Tributes and Retrospectives

Agnès Varda's body of work has been celebrated through tributes and retrospectives worldwide. Esteemed film festivals such as Cannes paid homage to her exceptional career. Retrospectives of her films highlighted the enduring impact of her work on contemporary cinema.

This chapter invites you to discover Agnès Varda's persistent and thoughtful work in the later years of her career. Her creativity, commitment to cinematic art, and ability to evoke universal themes make her a filmmaker whose influence extends far beyond her years of active production.

Chapter 9: The Legacy of Agnès Varda

The Influence of her Work on Contemporary Filmmakers

Agnès Varda's body of work continues to wield a profound influence on contemporary filmmakers worldwide. In this chapter, we will delve into how her contributions have left an indelible mark on modern cinema, inspiring new generations of filmmakers.

Exploring the Human Condition

Agnès Varda was renowned for her profound exploration of the human condition. Her authentic and empathetic approach to characters and human emotions paved the way for a new method of storytelling in cinema. Contemporary filmmakers draw inspiration from her ability to capture the complexity of daily life and human relationships.

Cinematic Revolution

As a pivotal figure in the New Wave movement, Agnès Varda contributed to a cinematic revolution that redefined the language of film. Her use of lightweight cameras, incorporation of non-professional actors, and exploration of innovative narrative forms have influenced many contemporary filmmakers seeking to push the boundaries of the medium.

Diversity of Styles and Genres

Agnès Varda explored a wide array of cinematic styles and genres throughout her career, seamlessly transitioning from documentary to experimental film and fiction. Her artistic versatility has inspired contemporary filmmakers to explore different realms and challenge cinematic conventions.

Perpetuity of her Impact on Cinema

Agnès Varda's impact on cinema endures, with her work being studied, celebrated, and showcased globally. Her films regularly feature in film festivals, retrospectives dedicated to her, and her artistic legacy is carefully preserved for future generations.

This chapter invites you to explore Agnès Varda's enduring legacy and understand how her work continues to influence and inspire contemporary filmmakers. Her distinctive approach to cinema, unwavering commitment to the human truth, and constant exploration of new artistic frontiers establish her as a timeless figure in the cinematic world.

Chapter 10: Agnès Varda's Personal Life

Her Life Beyond Cinema, Including Family and Hobbies

Agnès Varda was more than just a renowned filmmaker; she was a complex individual with a rich and varied personal life. In this chapter, we will delve into aspects of her life outside of cinema, including her family, hobbies, and the elements that influenced her art.

Her Family: Unwavering Support

Family always served as a source of support and inspiration for Agnès Varda. Her husband, Jacques Demy, was himself a renowned director, and their relationship influenced their respective works. Their artistic collaboration and shared love for cinema marked both their personal and professional lives.

Her Hobbies: Photography and Art

Outside of cinema, Agnès Varda had other artistic passions, notably photography and visual art. Her practice of photography often found a place in her films, adding a unique visual dimension to her work. Her artistic hobbies contributed to nurturing her creativity and shaping her cinematic aesthetic.

Personal Elements Influencing her Art

Agnès Varda frequently drew from her own life and personal experiences to fuel her art. Her reflections on love, loss, motherhood, and the passage of time were deeply influenced by her own life experiences. These personal elements added a touch of authenticity and intimacy to her cinematic work.

This chapter invites you to discover Agnès Varda's personal life beyond her illustrious cinematic career. Her relationships, passions, and personal experiences contributed to shaping her art in a unique way, enriching the depth of her cinematic oeuvre.

Chapter 11: The Legend of Agnès Varda

Legendary Anecdotes and Stories from Her Career

Agnès Varda's career is adorned with anecdotes and legendary stories that speak to her fascinating personality and creative genius. In this chapter, we will explore some of these anecdotes that have contributed to forging her legend in the world of cinema.

The Real-Time Filming of "Cléo de 5 à 7"

During the shooting of "Cléo de 5 à 7," Agnès Varda decided to follow the film's heroine, Cléo, in real-time for two hours. This bold decision required meticulous planning and perfect synchronization to capture the reality of each moment. The result became emblematic of her innovative approach to cinema.

The Documentary "Les Glaneurs et la Glaneuse"

Agnès Varda directed this poignant documentary about people who gather discarded objects and food. The film became a symbol of her commitment to society's forgotten and opened a dialogue about consumption and waste.

The Journey to Cuba for "Salut les Cubains"

Agnès Varda traveled to Cuba to make her documentary "Salut les Cubains," documenting the Cuban revolution. She faced political and logistical challenges to capture the daily life of Cubans. The film became a precious testimony to that historical period.

Landmark Moments in Her Life

Beyond her cinematic career, Agnès Varda experienced significant personal moments. The birth of her daughter, Rosalie Varda, was a joyful event that also influenced her work, notably in "Documenteur" (1981). The challenges and triumphs of her life were woven into her filmography in a unique way.

This chapter invites you to discover the legend of Agnès Varda through anecdotes and landmark moments from her career and personal life. These iconic stories reveal the extraordinary talent and fascinating personality of this legendary filmmaker.

CONCLUSION

Agnès Varda, an icon of French cinema and a symbol of the New Wave, leaves behind an invaluable cinematic legacy. Her exceptional artistic journey, marked by boundless creativity and a profound commitment to human truth, has left an indelible mark on the history of cinema.

With a career spanning over six decades, Agnès Varda explored a diversity of cinematic genres, from documentary to fiction to experimental cinema. Her work was characterized by a bold exploration of universal themes such as the human condition, self-discovery, and the ephemeral nature of life.

Her impact on cinema extends beyond her outstanding artistic achievements. Agnès Varda also paved the way for many female filmmakers, demonstrating a feminist sensibility and a commitment to women's rights that permeated her work. Her ability to push the boundaries of cinema made her a pioneer in the medium, and her influence on contemporary filmmakers is undeniable.

The prestigious awards and honors she received, including the Palme d'Honneur at Cannes, the César d'Honneur, and the Honorary Oscar, testify to the recognition of her impact on global cinema. She opened new horizons and inspired generations of filmmakers to rethink how stories are told on screen.

Agnès Varda's enduring legacy lives on through future generations of filmmakers who draw inspiration from her creativity, commitment, and passion for cinematic art. Her influence on contemporary cinema remains palpable, and her films continue to be celebrated through retrospectives and tributes worldwide.

Agnès Varda, with her legendary cinematic career and exceptional contribution to the seventh art, will forever remain a source of inspiration for those who cherish the power of cinema to capture the beauty, complexity, and authenticity of human life. Her legacy will endure, illuminating the path for those aspiring to tell stories with the same passion and artistic integrity she embodied throughout her life.

Appendix: Timeline of the Life and Work of Agnès Varda

This timeline traces key moments in the life and work of the filmmaker Agnès Varda, highlighting her cinematic achievements and significant career milestones.

- **May 30, 1928:** Agnès Varda is born in Ixelles, Belgium.
- **1954:** Directs her first short film, "La Pointe Courte," considered one of the precursors to the New Wave.
- **1961:** "Cléo de 5 à 7" receives critical acclaim, establishing Agnès Varda as a major director of the New Wave.
- **1962:** Creates the experimental short film "La Jetée."

- **1965:** Releases the film "Le Bonheur," sparking controversy due to its bold treatment of themes such as adultery.
- **1985:** "Vagabond" (Sans toit ni loi) wins the Palme d'Or at the Cannes Film Festival, solidifying Agnès Varda's stature as a major filmmaker.
- **2000:** Receives the Honorary César for her outstanding career.
- **2008:** Releases "The Beaches of Agnès," an autobiographical documentary praised by critics.
- **2015:** Agnès Varda is awarded the Palme d'Honneur at the Cannes Film Festival, becoming the first woman to receive this honor.
- **2017:** Receives an Honorary Oscar for her exceptional contribution to cinema.
- **2019:** Agnès Varda passes away at the age of 90, leaving behind a lasting cinematic legacy.

This timeline highlights key moments in the life and career of Agnès Varda, a filmmaker whose impact on French and global cinema continues to be felt and celebrated.